THE GOALSGUY®

GOAL SETTING 101

An Easy, Step-by-Step Guide
for Setting and Achieving a Goal

GARY RYAN BLAIR

THE
GOALSGUY

This book is dedicated to those

beginning the journey and

those renewing the fundamentals.

I hope the words on these pages

provide direction and inspiration

for your success!

Contents

Introduction Letter _____ **4**

1. The Fundamentals of Success _____ **6**

- Understand the Definition of "Goal" 7
- Know Why Goal Setting is Important 7
- Develop a Vision 8
- Create a Mission Statement 8
- Study the Anatomy of a Goal 9
- Accept Your Power of Choice 10
- Respect Reality – Face the Facts 11
- Be Authentic 11
- Cover the Ten Crucial Life Dimensions 12
- Make Everything Count 13
- Respect Your Rights and Responsibilities 14
- Ask the Six Important Goal Setting Questions 14

2. Plan Your Way to Success _____ **16**

- Know The Purpose of Planning 17
- Fit Plans to Circumstances 17
- Practice Spontaneity 18
- Start With Personal Planning 18
- Never Stop Planning 19
- Write Down Your Goals 19
- Do Your Reconnaissance 20
- Be Prepared 20
- Get Buy-In 21
- Create Contingency Plans 22
- Don't Forget Murphy's Law 22
- Use SWOT Analysis 23

3. Execute Your Way to Success _____ 25

- Act Like a Leader 26
- Practice Speed, Simplicity, and Boldness 26
- Only Results Matter 27
- Go The Extra Mile 27
- Always Set a Deadline 28
- Implement Now – Perfect Later 28
- Focus! Focus! Focus! 28
- Accent Execution – Go Forward 29
- Keep Moving 29
- Remain Flexible 30
- Be Unreasonable 30
- Watch Your Language 31

4. Manage Your Way to Success _____ 33

- Keep a Positive Attitude 34
- Work Economically 34
- Know Your Limits 34
- Set Performance Standards 35
- Find a Mentor 36
- Inspect What You Expect 36
- Don't Be Defeated 37
- Learn to Manage Fear 37
- Learn to Manage Failure and Setbacks 38
- Maintain Momentum 38
- Celebrate Your Accomplishments 39
- Have Fun 39

The Goal Setting 101 Training Program _____ 41

The GoalsGuy Library _____ 42

The GOALSGUY _____ 44

Dear Friend,

Achievement and accomplishment are among the most satisfying pleasures of all. Winning a race, beating the competition to market with a new idea, ridding yourself of a bad habit – these give delight and define success.

Achievements and accomplishments do not happen accidentally. They are the result of clearly defined goals acted upon until completion. Goals determine what you will or will not become or accomplish.

To be or not to be is directly related to your ability to set or not to set a goal!

Careful planning, thoughtful strategy, and faithful execution are the factors that lead to success. Success happens only when a clear, definable target has been established. Before taking action, you need a goal. We don't say, "Ready, Aim, Fire!" for nothing.

Goal Setting 101 addresses the fundamentals of setting and achieving a goal. My purpose in writing this book was to put the cookies of understanding on the lower shelf, within reach of anyone at any age. This book is about *achieving* your goals, and we're starting on the bunny hill.

Your primary interest in establishing a goal is to move yourself from where you are to where you want to be and to accomplish more than you thought possible. My goal in writing this book is to offer goal setting methods, insights and suggestions to those seeking their signature path to success. View these lessons as the fundamentals that work. Your goal should include becoming master of the fundamentals.

Goal Setting 101's self-paced format encourages you to become personally involved. Be sure read this book with a pen and highlighter in hand. It takes study and practice to produce good results. But the efforts required will prove to be minor when measured against the payoffs!

I wish I had read a book like this when I was younger. I am confident I would have achieved more throughout my life with less wasted effort and with fewer bumps and bruises that I know call experience.

The lessons in *Goal Setting 101* work. They do not promise or provide a quick fix, but with diligent effort toward the achievement of your goals, your results can be substantial.

In a rapid-fire presentation, this book introduces you to the fundamentals of goal setting. It explains how you must think, plan, execute, manage, and eventually celebrate your way to success.

Goal Setting 101 is separated into bite-sized portions, packed with a powerhouse of information. It is most effective when read from cover to cover in order. This is a logical step-by-step journey of what it takes to set and achieve a goal. Each section is important – each one counts.

My overriding ambition is that one day, not long from now, learning how to set and achieve a goal will be as common as learning how to operate your microwave.

My goal is simply to help you achieve yours, so let's get busy and learn to master the fundamentals of goal setting.

Everything Counts!

Gary Ryan Blair
Gary Ryan Blair
The GoalsGuy

P.S. I welcome your comments. Please drop a note to me at gary@goalsguy.com and
    share your thoughts on *Goal Setting 101.*

1 The Fundamentals of Success

Here are 12 fundamentals that you must become intimately aware of if you are to realize your personal definition of success:

- **Understand the Definition of "Goal"**

- **Know Why Goal Setting is Important**

- **Develop a Vision**

- **Create a Mission Statement**

- **Study the Anatomy of a Goal**

- **Accept Your Power of Choice**

- **Respect Reality – Face the Facts**

- **Be Authentic**

- **Cover the Ten Crucial Life Dimensions**

- **Make Everything Count**

- **Respect Your Rights and Responsibilities**

- **Ask the Six Important Goal Setting Questions**

At the end of this chapter, you will find the first of the four exercises in this book: Identify the Goals. Use this exercise to help you distinguish effective, productive goal statements from ineffective attempts.

■ Understand the Definition of "Goal"

"A goal is an end toward which you direct specific effort."

In this context, the "end" is an exact and tangible result you want and for which you are willing to expend effort in order to achieve. The amount and intensity of effort provided is always dependent on the individual and how important the goal is to that person.

The three key elements of a goal are:

- **An accomplishment to be achieved**

- **A measurable outcome**

- **A specific date and time to accomplish the goal**

Therefore, a goal is a specific, measurable accomplishment to be achieved within a specific time frame.

■ Know Why Goal Setting is Important

The benefits of goal setting are neither imaginary nor vague. There are meaningful values to be gained from practical goal setting.

- Goals establish direction for your life. If you never set a goal, how will you know where you are going?

- Goals identify results. If no goal exists, how do you measure your progress?

- Goals challenge you to grow. If you never set a goal, how do you move out of your comfort zone?

- Goal setting improves your self-image. It improves you today and makes you feel better for tomorrow.

- Goal setting gives you confidence. Your frustration is immediately lowered when vagueness and doubt are replaced by focus and concentration.

- Goal setting forces you to be specific. It is the first positive, obvious step to success.

■ Develop a Vision

A vision is a way of seeing or conceiving what you want to create or achieve. The single most important thing to have before you do any planning is a vision. How can you plan without knowing what you envision for your life? It would be like starting a trip without first determining your destination, purpose of the trip, and what you expect to do when you get there.

For your vision to be translated to action, it must be shared with the people who will be impacted by it. People cannot help you achieve your vision unless they know and understand why your vision is important.

You must walk the talk. It is essential that your vision be understood, shared, accepted, and lived by everyone who plays a role in making it a reality.

Boil down your vision and your goals. Find the fewest and best words to express what you want. This will save time, remove confusion, and minimize error.

■ Create a Mission Statement

If a goal is a specific, measurable, and time-bound accomplishment that you want to achieve, then a mission is an umbrella under which you place your goals and related actions.

A mission statement interprets "reason for being;" it enables you to clarify your purpose for yourself and others who are interested.

A mission statement is a declaration of who you are, why you exist, and what you intend to accomplish.

In business, the organizational mission answers the big question: "What is our business?" In personal planning, the question is "What is my life's business?" In both cases, the answer must define the reason for being.

Why do you exist? If you can't answer that question, you can't develop an effective plan that can feed what you need in order to continue to exist.

We all have to give meaning to our lives. We must find or create reasons for living!

■ Study the Anatomy of a Goal

Anatomy of a Goal

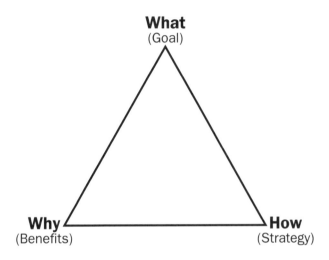

Three collaborators are involved with every goal: the what, the why, and the how. Each has a different role to play with a separate yet collaborative reason for participation.

- **The "what" is the goal, which provides direction.**
- **The "why" is the set of personal benefits, which provides fuel to reach the goal.**
- **The "how" is the map that provides the mile markers for achievement.**

■ Accept Your Power of Choice

As your birthright, you are given your greatest power – the power to choose. Every moment offers you a choice: to exercise this power by setting and holding a direction or to veer off course. Every choice counts! There are no insignificant choices, no neutral actions. Even the smallest gesture has a consequence, leading you toward or away from your goals.

Success is the intentional, pre-meditated use of choice and decision. Unless you choose – with certainty – what it is you want, you accept table scraps by default!

You are born with great capabilities, but you will not achieve your potential until you call upon yourself to fulfill it. You may rise to the occasion when it presents itself, but to assure self-fulfillment, you must provide occasions to rise to.

Clearly defined goals allow you to travel toward another horizon that represents the end of one experience and the transition to a new and better existence. The objective is to choose the right goals, and then to create the necessary causes – the effects will follow.

The difference between what one person and another achieves depends more on goal choices than on abilities. The profound differences between successful people and others are the goals they choose to pursue. Individuals with similar talents, intelligence, and abilities will achieve different results because they select and pursue different goals.

No decision is difficult to make… if you get all the facts!

■ Respect Reality – Face the Facts

The truth will prevail, one way or another and usually sooner rather than later. It is better to face facts at the planning phase, and to convince others to do the same. This is not for the sake of building character or maintaining mortality. It is a matter of survival. Whether or not you face it, truth will create consequences.

True and accurate information is essential to your success. Whether or not you *like* that information is irrelevant, the quality and integrity of information is what counts. What you need is integrity of data and the willingness to operate with it. It is essential to understand that reality isn't necessarily going to be the way you wish things to be or the way they seem to be; reality is the way things actually are.

Get this and you've got it: Reality moves you toward your goals; denial moves you away. Denial is self-imposed deception, convenient cover, yet a poor alibi. Denying reality, for any reason, leads only to stress and frustration and takes you away from your goals. Period!

■ Be Authentic

You must be able to identify success or you won't have any way of monitoring your progress or knowing if you have achieved your goals.

If success fell out of the sky and hit you on top of the head, would you know what it was? If you cannot answer that question with clarity you may want to give it some thought.

"Mirror, Mirror on the Wall…" Beware of the *Snow White* trap; the wicked witch can never be happy as long as she continued to compare herself to someone else. If a goal is truly your own, proceed happily without being sidetracked by the accomplishments of others. All too often, people pursue things that they see other people achieve.

It's all about ownership and authenticity. If a goal is truly your own, you will take pride in it. If it is a watered-down, hand-me-down from someone else's vision, you will forever experience a value conflict.

■ Cover the Ten Crucial Life Dimensions

"Values lay the groundwork for your goals. Goals lead to the fulfillment of your mission. Your mission leads to the realization of your life's work – your legacy."

Goals need to be set in each of the following ten categories:

- **Personal** — Goals relating to character development, personal growth, and practical living issues.

- **Health** — Goals relating to exercise, appearance, diet and overall health and well-being.

- **Recreation** — Goals relating to relaxation, renewal, hobbies, vacations, and leisure activities.

- **Family** — Goals relating to your partner, children, parents, and relatives.

- **Friends** — Goals such as expanding your circle of friends and enriching existing relationships.

- **Community** — Goals involving a commitment to serving others through your time, talents, heart, and possessions.

- **Career** — Goals relating to skill development, networking, current projects, and future ambitions.

- **Financial** — Goals relating to income growth, savings, investments, retirement, and estate planning.

- **Household** — Goals relating to household improvements, security, and general maintenance.

- **Spiritual** — Goals relating to faith, spiritual growth, and the strengthening of your beliefs.

■ Make Everything Count

"Everything Counts!" is a philosophy for living. Its meaning is simple, yet powerful: Every thought, decision, and action moves you closer to or further from your goals.

Self-knowledge grows as you subject your life to examination. Listening to your own speech, reflecting on your own thoughts, looking at your own actions – these are the processes by which you master yourself. You shape your philosophies and yourself by observing and striving to understand the events of each moment. A focus on virtues to attain and vices to forego is crucial.

Pursuit of your goals is compelling. Each step offers an opportunity for growth, learning, and self-improvement.

Just as chess has its rules, so does the game of life. And while knowing a game's rules does not guarantee that you'll win every match, disregarding the rules makes playing the game difficult and winning impossible.

The examined life is the one worth living. Make everything count!

■ Respect Your Rights and Responsibilities

You have...

- the right, privilege, responsibility, and honor to set and achieve a goal.
- the right to be successful, happy, and prosperous.
- the right to pursue your own individual path in life.
- a responsibility to follow through on all your commitments.
- a responsibility to teach and share what you have learned in life to others.
- a responsibility to become all that you are capable of becoming.

If you are serious about achieving your goals, respect your rights and responsibilities.

■ Ask the Six Important Goal Setting Questions

Consider the goal-setting process as an interview. When setting a goal and planning for its accomplishment, always ask the following six questions:

- **Who**
  Who will be involved in helping you achieve this goal?

- **What**
  What is the goal? What specifically do you want to accomplish?

- **Where**
  Where are you now in relation to this goal?

- **When**
  On what date do you expect to achieve this goal?

- **How**
  How will you accomplish this goal?

- **Why**
  Why do you want to achieve this goal?

Exercise #1: Identify the Goals

Look over the following list and select yes or no in the appropriate column whether you consider each item to be a goal.

	YES	NO
1. Increase sales and profits.	○	○
2. Lose 18 pounds by my birthday.	○	○
3. Manage work more effectively.	○	○
4. See the Grand Canyon on our upcoming June vacation.	○	○
5. Get a raise.	○	○
6. Get a better job.	○	○
7. Reduce clutter in the house.	○	○
8. Start my own business.	○	○
9. Score over 1200 on my SAT's next Saturday.	○	○
10. Buy a Car.	○	○

Answer: Only numbers 2, 4, and 9 can truly be considered goals. They are the only ones that meet the specific, measurable, and time-bound criteria of a goal. The remaining are wishes.

2 Plan Your Way to Success

There is simply no substitute for planning your way to success. Here are the critical 12 points you must understand and practice as you plan your way to success:

- **Know The Purpose of Planning**

- **Fit Plans to Circumstances**

- **Practice Spontaneity**

- **Start With Personal Planning**

- **Never Stop Planning**

- **Write Down Your Goals**

- **Do Your Reconnaissance**

- **Be Prepared**

- **Get Buy-In**

- **Create Contingency Plans**

- **Don't Forget Murphy's Law**

- **Use SWOT Analysis**

In "Exercise #2: SWOT–Strengths, Weaknesses, Opportunities, and Threats," you will gain practice with what is likely to be the best tool you will find for immediate and effective analysis of a given situation.

■ Know The Purpose of Planning

Whether you realize it or not, you are almost always involved in planning. It might be as simple as planning for a birthday party or something more complex. Whatever you do in life requires some degree of planning, consciously or unconsciously.

- Plans help you analyze where you are and can point the way to where you want to be.
- Plans help you determine the career you might want to go into and the best way to enter and conduct that career.
- Plans help you operate your career or business and can be used to raise money and enhance credibility.
- Plans inform everyone around you that you are a person with a purpose.
- Planning projects expectations and the direction you are taking.
- Planning ensures the buy-in from others that will be affected by a plan's outcome.
- Plans are a means to monitor performance.

■ Fit Plans to Circumstances

One does not plan and then try to make circumstances fit those plans. One tries to make plans fit the circumstances. The difference between success and failure depends on the ability, or lack of it, to do just that.

The effective goal setter is not content to make the most of what happens to come his way. They devise, invent, and create situations tailored to their strengths. This is the essence of proactivity: creating circumstances rather than merely responding to them.

■ Practice Spontaneity

Part of achieving a goal is being sensitive and open to what fortune and circumstance have to offer and taking advantage of these opportunities when they present themselves–not before and, certainly, not after.

Value spontaneity. Goal setting involves establishing a delicate balance between planning and improvisation. What should never be left to chance, however, is the ability to execute any plan. Logistics, support, and training should be thoroughly fixed and completely reliable.

■ Start With Personal Planning

What you want out of life, the quality of your life, should be reflected in your planning. Answering the following questions (along with others like them) will provide you with a working platform, the foundation that all of your goals will stand upon. Your initial step is to build a platform of choice, not simply to accept what life throws at you by chance!

- What do you want out of life?
- How much money do you want to earn?
- How many hours do you want to spend working?
- Do you want to watch your kids grow up?
- Ideally where would you like to live?
- How long a commute to work would you accept?

It is essential to know what your working platform is in order to develop purposeful goals. If you work for someone other than yourself, you must know what you want before you can know if your job can give it to you.

You will experience a sense of "Eureka!" when you begin goal setting with personal planning.

Never Stop Planning

Planning must be done, analyzed, re-planned, and done again. Most people plan on an annual basis, but there is nothing sacred about this time. The following are things that trigger immediate review and possible re-planning:

- An action by a competitor
- A major change in the marketplace
- Loss of any type
- A new and unexpected threat from the economy
- Financial struggles
- Current strategies that aren't working
- A change in personal needs
- Maturity – seeing things from a different point of view

Write Down Your Goals

Your goals gain credibility and clout through the process of writing. You increase the probability of achieving a goal when you write it down.

Writing something down is the first step toward achieving it. There's something about putting something down on paper that forces you to get down to specifics. It's harder to deceive yourself or anyone else when your idea is exposed on paper.

There is only one exception to this rule: It's when you have a major goal and nothing else could possibly stand in its way. It's clear and compelling, and it continually propels you towards achievement. It calls out to you, and you can't help but think, dream, and act upon it. You unconsciously know what to do to get it done.

Don't make the mistake of thinking you can keep your goals in your head. For goal setting to have any value, goals must be written down. Only by writing each step can you see where you are going. Similarly, writing down your goals also enables you to look back to determine if you have done what you planned to do!

■ Do Your Reconnaissance

You can never have too much reconnaissance. Use every means available before, during, and after you have achieved the goal. **Information must be facts, not opinions, negative as well as positive.** Information is like eggs, the fresher the better.

Insist on basing plans and decisions on facts gathered at firsthand or as close as possible to firsthand. Determine what you need to know, determine how to obtain what you need to know, and have good reason for wanting the information in the first place. Then, and only then, will you truly know what you know and what you don't know, so that you can base actions, plans and decisions on a foundation of firm fact.

Pay attention to the dozens of unglamorous support items that are necessary to your success, and be certain that they are in place and ready to go before the endeavor is launched. Don't put off routine tasks.

■ Be Prepared

Devote time to preparations directly related to an operation or goal. Committing resources to a poorly prepared project is a waste of time and resource.

Planning saves 10 to 1 in execution. Momentum is essential to goal attainment, and planning is the starter.

If you start preparing yourself and making decisions the day after you graduate about where you want to work and what you want to do, odds are you'll find yourself underemployed, underpaid, and undervalued. Or worse, unemployed.

Prepare well, deeply and thoroughly, in advance!

Get Buy-In

When attempting to achieve a goal that involves others, be sure that everyone is singing from the same sheet of music. This does not mean stamping out individual initiative, but it does mean agreeing on common goals and subordinating to the achievement of these any personal disharmonies or disagreements.

Everyone involved in achieving the goal should have a part in establishing it. Participation in the goal-setting process helps ensure that the goal will be successfully accomplished, because people have bought into its importance and method of achievement.

The way to establish buy-in is to create a sense of ownership in the affected individuals. There are two ways to create a true sense of ownership. You can incorporate some of the individual into what you are creating, or you can incorporate some of what you are creating into the individual.

For buy-in to take place, there has to be a transfer, either from the individual to the goal or from the goal into the individual. Create a forum for input and warm the other party to your idea in a natural and acceptable manner.

The most important ingredient in motivation is knowledge of goals, objectives, and purpose. You cannot expect blind obedience. The first step toward getting buy-in is defining objectives and then making those objectives clear to the people who will be impacted by the goal. Communicate those objectives persuasively so that everyone involved will feel that they have a stake in the achievement of the goal.

Successful buy-in involves a three-step analysis:

- **Discussion** – Discuss the who, what, where, when, how, and why of the desired goal.

- **Compromise** – Encourage give-and-take between parties. The compromise and negotiation of the goal are part of the achievement process.

- **Agreement** – Seek the settlement of the goal, achievement process, and assigned responsibilities.

Discussion, compromise, and agreement require that all parties interact with one another during the goal-setting process. This interaction means that people must talk, the most essential element in the early stages of goal setting is communication.

■ Create Contingency Plans

Contingency means something that is likely but not certain to happen. Every plan deals with what you expect to happen. But no matter how well you plan, the unexpected can and often does take place. Sometimes favorable, sometimes unfavorable.

You can't possibly plan for every contingency. However, in critical areas of your plan it is in your best interest to build three levels of projections. The three projections you should make in critical areas are:

- The most likely–What you think will actually happen.
- The least likely–The worst case you can imagine for what you are projecting.
- The most optimistic–The best possible scenario you can imagine if everything goes beyond your expectations.

When it comes to contingency planning, an ounce of prevention is worth a pound of cure!

■ Don't Forget Murphy's Law

Sometimes – and far more often than any of us wish – things will go wrong!

There are a variety of nagging occurrences that require you to put back-up systems (such as always backing up the computer or having an alternative means of transportation) in place. Murphy has an uncanny way of making surprise visits.

■ Use SWOT Analysis

The SWOT analysis is perhaps the best tool you will find for immediate and effective analysis of a given situation. SWOT stands for *Strengths, Weaknesses, Opportunities,* and *Threats.*

There are two variations of a SWOT analysis and each should be examined before any actions taken.

- **Internal SWOT Analysis**

  The circumstances, objectives, and conditions that surround you personally and or professionally.

- **External SWOT Analysis**

  The circumstances, objectives, and conditions of the situation in which you are competing.

The external environment is not something you can control. However, knowing what you face gives you the ability to anticipate and adjust accordingly.

■ **Exercise #2**
SWOT – Strengths, Weaknesses, Opportunities, and Threats

Select a goal you would like to achieve and then complete an internal SWOT analysis. This will provide you with a quick and effective analysis of the goal.

Goal: _____

Strengths _____

_____

_____

Weaknesses _____

_____

_____

Opportunities _____

_____

_____

Threats _____

_____

_____

3 Execute Your Way to Success

Action is the conduit through which advancement flows. In this section, you'll get acquainted with the 12 keys to implementing your plan:

- **Act Like a Leader**

- **Practice Speed, Simplicity, and Boldness**

- **Only Results Matter**

- **Go The Extra Mile**

- **Always Set a Deadline**

- **Implement Now – Perfect Later**

- **Focus! Focus! Focus!**

- **Accent Execution – Go Forward**

- **Keep Moving**

- **Remain Flexible**

- **Be Unreasonable**

- **Watch Your Language**

Exercise #3: Traits and Characteristics offers a proven process that will help you to determine your goals by prompting you to examine your likes, dislikes, strengths, and weaknesses.

■ Act Like a Leader

What does a leader do? A leader leads! You have no choice but to lead yourself in the direction of your goals, no one else will do the job for you.

The first rule of personal leadership is to act as if you are a leader – because you are. No hesitation, no discussion – just lead. It's easier to lead than to push. You've got to know what is going on all the time. You cannot swim without being in the water. You cannot skate without being on the ice. The only way to achieve a goal is to lead yourself to victory.

The primary criterion of any leader is the ability to achieve the goal, whatever it may be. Build your life on a permanent record of accomplishment.

The debate as to whether leaders are born or made is bogus. The truth is that some leaders are made, but *most leaders make themselves*. How? They believe in themselves and act like leaders!

■ Practice Speed, Simplicity, and Boldness

A plan or course of action driven by speed, simplicity, and boldness is difficult to fault. In most circumstances, these three qualities are reliable yardsticks against which any idea may be measured.

Implementation is everything and it better be fast. These days it's far better to be 80 percent right and quick than 100 percent and three months late.

All statements of mission and vision should be simple, no matter how complex the goal may be. But simplicity is only possible if you thoroughly understand your mission, purpose, objectives, and goals.

Act in a way that recognizes that any action has potentially momentous consequences, the full import of which will not be immediately apparent. The goal? Make boldness a matter of routine.

The best ideas typically have a short shelf life. In life, many circumstances conspire to retard progress. Act as quickly as you can. Complex plans often look appealing on paper, but tend to fall apart in execution. Keep your plans as simple as possible. Always consider the bolder course!

■ Only Results Matter

Theatrics are hollow in the absence of results. Don't mistake the *show* of leadership, no matter how necessary, for leadership itself.

Leadership is a synthesis of theory and practice, of preparation and spontaneity, of rehearsal and improvisation.

You are not only the source of direction for your goal; you are its chief example as well.

Results are judge and jury. In the long run, it's what you do, not what you say, that will destroy you. Do the right thing. Ultimately, our actions are of greater consequence than our words. In critical situations, telling people what they want to hear may provide temporary relief. In the long run, however, this approach will not avert disaster.

Say what needs to be said; then, act accordingly. **Temporary discomfort is better than temporary relief – if it averts permanent catastrophe.**

■ Go The Extra Mile

Do more than is required! What is the distance between someone who achieves their goals consistently and those who spend their lives and careers merely following? The extra mile. Advancement only comes with habitually doing more than you are asked.

■ Always Set a Deadline

Without a strict deadline, a challenging but reachable goal that is qualified completely remains too nebulous. The lack of a specific deadline often results in a lack of focused approach to attaining your goal. A clear idea to the degree to which you must marshal your energies does not exist, because the goal is open-ended.

No Timeline = No Commitment! The litmus test of commitment is a clearly understood deadline. If you are unable or unwilling to establish a deadline for your goal, you probably need to examine your commitment.

■ Implement Now – Perfect Later

You cannot afford to wait for perfect conditions. Goal setting is often a matter of balancing timing against available resources. Opportunities are easily lost while waiting for perfect conditions.

Everyone must make one major concession to the real world, and that is simply that it is the real world. In theory and in games, there is a right time to decide and take action. In the real world, however, there is no totally right time. You cannot control everything. Nor can you wait for the roll of the dice to come out just right. Sometimes you have to play with the cards you have. Make this fundamental pact with reality—or reality will leave you in the dust.

■ Focus! Focus! Focus!

Never stop thinking about your goal! A decision to achieve a goal is never made just once, it happens continuously. A goal requires a focused commitment of energy.

All successful goal setters know above all else, what they are doing. They know what the goal or goals are. They focus all activity on achieving those goals and do not allow themselves to get distracted.

■ Accent Execution – Go Forward

Your job is not done when you have answered **what** is to be done. You must also answer **how** it is to be done. Plans are nothing if they cannot be executed successfully.

To go forward is a recognition that life is dynamic, not static. To go forward is to make each move, each action, count. To go forward is to give up dwelling on the past.

There are no new battles to be won. Your job is to commit your past successes and failures to memory and apply their lessons to present situations. Apply is the operative word. Use the past to go forward. Experience and knowledge of the past are useful to you insofar as they can be applied to the present and to the future.

Go forward. Move quickly. But go forward and move quickly with all the preparation necessary to ensure an efficient and profitable result – not just a wasteful flurry of action. There is no speed limit on the road to success!

Goals never fail – only implementation does. Take decisive action with a maximum effort. Lukewarm measures tip your hand toward mediocrity.

■ Keep Moving

The winning attitude is one of movement and progress, not digging in and holding ground. Defensive postures are illusions. Digging in may make you feel safe, but, in reality, you have transformed yourself into a stationary target. **In any competitive enterprise, action is preferable to inaction.**

As the cliché goes, "the best defense is a good offense." Go forward... be aggressive. Don't give your fears or competition a chance to pin you down. Trepidation and loss of confidence come with a defensive posture. Attack the problem, attack the market, attack the competition, and you are proceeding positively. Fear will melt and confidence will rise!

■ Remain Flexible

When you initiate action on your written goals, a funny thing seems to almost always happen. Some timelines begin to appear unrealistic, because factors change. Sometimes you find that achievement will take you longer than you imagined. At other times, the timeline gets shorter.

At any rate, once you get going, factors that you could not have anticipated often emerge. It's important to understand that goals can and do change as well, although I'm not giving you a free meal ticket to shift things around for purposes of mere convenience.

■ Be Unreasonable

Be uncompromising in areas that permit no compromise, such as issues of quality, concentration, and follow through. In the truly important matters, do not hesitate to ask for a great deal from yourself and from the people around you. You will discover new levels of performance. But you have to demand and expect it!

When you have gone just as far as you can go, you can still go a little bit further.

Set the bar high – higher than even you think reality warrants – and challenge yourself to clear it.

Nothing of any lasting value was ever created by someone who was reasonable. It is the unreasonable people, those discontented with the status quo, the dreamers and visionaries who nevertheless have their feet planted firmly on solid ground who improve people's lives and advance society.

Reasonable people can talk themselves out of anything, no matter how great the merit of the goal. If anyone tells you to be reasonable – run, don't just walk, away!

Successful people do what unsuccessful people simply won't or can't do. And in so doing, they frequently achieve the impossible.

■ Watch Your Language

Here are some effective phrases you should say and think. Carefully chosen words, spoken in affirmative language bolster confidence while pursuing goals.

- I can!
- I will!
- I choose to do this!
- I am responsible!
- I'm up to the challenge!
- Give it to me; I'll get it done!
- You can count on me!
- Consider it done!
- I'm on top of it!
- You've come to the right place!
- Let's get started!
- It's a done deal!
- I give you my word!

An effective goal setter will never express an *opinion*! You *know* and speak as if you know! Everything that comes out of your mouth should be without doubt. *You can be wrong, but never be in doubt.* If there is any doubt or fear in your voice, you and others around you will feel it and cave in.

Examine your speech! You can and will inspire confidence with your words and vocal tone. This is accomplished, in part, by making positive, direct, unqualified statements. Base what you say on accurate information. Get the facts!

Don't pooh-pooh away the importance of what you've just read. Consider this, if you asked two people the same question and the first one replied, " I'll try to get it done." and the second person replied, "You can count on me to get it done!" which person would you be more inclined to believe?

The moral of this story? Watch your language!

■ Exercise # 3: Traits and Characteristics

The following is a proven process that will help you to determine your goals. It involves triggering goals by making a list of your likes, dislikes, strengths, and weaknesses. Write answers to each characteristic below:

Likes _____

Dislikes _____

Strengths _____

Weaknesses _____

After completing the exercise, cross-reference your likes with your strengths and your dislikes with your weaknesses. When you link the pairs together you are likely to find goals waiting for you. Things that you like to do and are good at certainly point the way to positive activities. The opposite is also true; dislikes and weaknesses should be avoided.

4 Manage Your Way to Success

Goals aren't usually attained "overnight," so managing the journey to success is a critical aspect of achievement. Here are a dozen rules for keeping you on track:

- **Keep a Positive Attitude**

- **Work Economically**

- **Know Your Limits**

- **Set Performance Standards**

- **Find a Mentor**

- **Inspect What You Expect**

- **Don't Be Defeated**

- **Learn to Manage Fear**

- **Learn to Manage Failure and Setbacks**

- **Maintain Momentum**

- **Celebrate Your Accomplishments**

- **Have Fun**

The final exercise in this book, "Top Ten Goals" asks you to put what you've learned about goal setting and achievement to work by clearly stating the ten goals you most want to pursue now.

■ Keep a Positive Attitude

Success is an attitude. True, success at any given moment may be measured by sales figures, revenue, and profits. But, in the long run, success is an attitude. It is a winning attitude that motivates success, and it is a winning attitude that sustains success.

Only by stretching do we grow. If you push the limits, you define new limits. And then you should push those. You are capable of producing and achieving much more than you believe possible.

Expect reverses, expect losses, and expect rejection. They are inevitable. But why give them the last word? Take them as bumps in the road to success!

■ Work Economically

Maximum productivity is not the same as working continuously or working to exhaustion. **Maximum productivity is working economically.** It is managing time and resources efficiently.

Know when to move – and know when to rest and to prepare to move. You cannot afford to squander precious human resources on creating the mere appearance of non-stop productivity.

■ Know Your Limits

Know the limits of what you can expect from yourself and those around you. Be willing to push those limits, but understand that pushing beyond them is subject to one of the few absolute laws of life that govern human nature: the law of diminishing returns.

Pushed beyond limits, people work inefficiently, poorly, and even counterproductively. Know – and respect – your limits!

■ Set Performance Standards

Performance standards indicate the level of results expected for each goal. Standards of performance serve two primary purposes:

- They indicate progress made toward the goal.
- They determine when the goal has been achieved.

It is imperative that these standards be established before any activities begin. They represent specific objectives and milestones to be reached. Specific times must be established to indicate when progress will be measured.

Five separate standards for performance should be established:

- **Outstanding**
  Greater progress was achieved at the milestone mark.

- **Good**
  Progress is on target or just a little ahead of schedule.

- **Average**
  Progress made is somewhat consistent during the time allotted.

- **Poor**
  Progress is below acceptable levels.

- **Counter-Productive**
  No progress and current activities are impeding other areas.

For example, if your goal is to lose 20 pounds within the next four months, standards of performance might be as follows:

8 pounds lost within 30 days = Outstanding

6 pounds lost within 30 days = Good

5 pounds lost within 30 days = Average

2 pounds lost within 30 days = Poor

1 pound gained within 30 days = Counterproductive

■ Find a Mentor

Surround yourself with people whose knowledge and judgment you trust; then, make good use of them. **Effective goal setting is consultative; it does not squander – it leverages – all available brainpower.** Welcome and actively seek multiple perspectives on any given problem.

Value experience above all else. Acquire it actively for yourself. Seek it out in others. In planning, resort to the books only after you have consulted with people who have actually done and lived through the tasks you are contemplating. Never close yourself to suggestion and insight from others.

■ Inspect What You Expect

Achieving your goals requires careful periodic monitoring of the actions taken and the measurable results of those actions.

Inspecting your goals is the exact same process you go through when examining the expiration date on the milk container in your refrigerator. You expect it to be fresh and good; if not, you dump it. The same can be said for the 3000-mile check-up you put your car through. You invest a little bit of time and energy now to inspect what you expect; by neglecting this critical task, you pay a lot more later on.

Inspecting expectations confirms that time and efforts are productive in achieving the intended results. The performance standards established early on set the stage for the inspection process. You should establish clear and precise calendar dates for review.

You need to ensure that what you want done gets done!

Relentlessly and repeatedly review procedures and requirements to weed out anything that is nonessential or smacks of "make-work." Streamline wherever possible, always stopping short of compromising quality.

■ Don't Be Defeated

You will never lack for nay-sayers to tell you that all is lost or that you are beaten. Don't join the party! Exhaust all alternatives. **Victory and defeat are rarely absolutes.** There is a whole spectrum between these two extremes. Don't be in a hurry to call that gray area black. You gain nothing by speeding to such a conclusion.

■ Learn to Manage Fear

Everyone is afraid from time to time. The more intelligent you are, the more you may be frightened. The courageous person forces himself or herself, in spite of fear, to carry on. Discipline, pride, self-respect, self-confidence, and the love of victory are attributes that will make you courageous… even when you are afraid.

Don't deny your fears. Don't try to run away from them. Carry on in spite of them!

Learn to live with fear; learn to control it so that fear is never put in the driver's seat. You cannot learn to avoid fear, but you can learn to recognize when you are in danger of acting in blind accordance with it.

Everybody's afraid. Some are just more chicken than others. Your success depends on your ability to advance in the face of fear. Since when did being the underdog provide a good reason to quit?

Do not pass the buck, dodge duty, or transfer your load to someone else. Don't go looking for a free ride on the road of irresponsibility – it's a dead end.

The person who cannot face a fear will always be running from it. Better to run toward a goal than away from a fear.

There is a time to take council of fear, and there is a time to forget your fears. It is always important to know exactly what you are doing. The time to take council of your fears is just before you make an important decision. That is the time to listen to every fear you can imagine. When you have collected all of the facts and fears, make your decision. Once you make your decision, forget your fears, and move full steam ahead.

■ Learn to Manage Failure and Setbacks

Everyone fails. But that doesn't mean you must identify yourself as a failure. Failure applies to a situation, a particular time and place. If you don't let it devastate you, failure can be an opportunity: for learning, for recovery, for the creation and demonstration of character.

No one wins all the time. Learn to take your losses, learn from them if possible, and move on. The same is true for any goal involving risk. You cannot avoid failure all of the time, but you can refuse to be pinned down by it.

True success is character, and character is measured by how high you bounce when you topple from that height and hit bottom.

Failure is a part of life. It will happen. The worst failure, however, are those we declare without having exhausted all possibilities and alternatives. Do not be in a hurry to write off any goal or project. When something falters, intervene.

It takes courage and character to engage and follow through on a faltering project. It takes courage and character to be a success.

■ Maintain Momentum

Momentum is one of your most valuable resources. It takes a great deal of energy to overcome inertia – to get going – so, once you are on your way, it is your job to keep things going.

Focus yourself, and focus your resources. Resist the temptation to merely hold your ground or consolidate. Stoke the fires continuously. Maintain the energy!

■ Celebrate Your Accomplishments

Too few people take time for ceremonies, for occasions on which identity is formed, defined, and affirmed. And, when ceremonies are observed, they are too often carried out in a dull, hollow, perfunctory fashion.

If necessary, create occasions to celebrate.

Identify and credit exceptional achievement. This is crucial to reinforcing the level of productivity and quality you want and expect. Recognition celebrates achievement and builds confidence; it provides an incentive to further achievement. It is an indispensable self-management tool.

Become a great believer in the importance of celebration and rewards. Prompt positive reinforcement in the form of commemoration and celebration is essential to morale. Few people devote time to this.

It is always good to review and reinforce your accomplishments. Rewards should always point the way toward future performance.

Express your sincere appreciation of your performance. Your untiring effort has led you toward this success. When you meet adversity, the same spirit of devotion will make you confident and courageous. You should be proud of yourself.

The function of praise is to encourage continued superior performance while setting the bar a little higher. Be generous to yourself. It is often overlooked.

■ Have Fun

Humor is when an expected future is replaced with an unexpected future. The more unexpected the more humorous.

The road to success is often bumpy and constantly under construction, but that doesn't mean you can't enjoy the ride. You will and should be experiencing moments of deep satisfaction and fun. This is the best indicator to let you know that you are striving for something that is authentic and has genuine importance to you!

■ Exercise #4: Top Ten Goals

Remember where you started?

"A goal is an end toward which you direct specific effort."

The three key elements of a goal are:

- An accomplishment to be achieved

- A measurable outcome

- A specific date and time to accomplish the goal

Goal setting starts with a pad of paper, a pen, and you. Write down your ten most important goals and then apply the lessons you have learned in the book to make them come true.

1. _____

2. _____

3. _____

4. _____

5. _____

6. _____

7. _____

8. _____

9. _____

10. _____

GOAL SETTING 101
TRAINING PROGRAM

Enhance the powerful message of *Goal Setting 101* with the one-day training program built around the handbook's hard-hitting message. Help all your employees understand how to set and achieve any goal.

GOAL SETTING 101

*An Easy, Step-by-Step Guide
for Setting and Achieving a Goal*

GARY RYAN BLAIR

GOALSGUY

Use *The Goal Setting 101 Training Program* to:

- **Lay the foundation for achieving team and company goals.**
- **Achieve a commanding competitive edge.**
- **Become an industry leader.**

The blend of lectures, group and individual discovery exercises, and open discussions give participants a well-rounded grasp of what it takes to set and achieve a goal. *Goal Setting 101* drives the message down to the grass-roots level. Everyone in the organization is assigned personal responsibility for building an extraordinary life and business.

For more information call 1-877-GOALSGUY

or visit us at www.GoalsGuy.com

GOALSGUY LIBRARY

	PRICE	QTY	TOTAL
...s? *Powerful Questions to Discover What You Want Out of Life*	$14.95		
...nts!: *A High-Velocity Formula for Maximum Achievement*	$7.95		
...r Bridge to The New Economy: *Ten Rules for Success in the Digital Age*	$7.95		
...s & Realities of Goal-Setting: *Guidelines for Designing an Extraordinary Life*	$7.95		
...ce & Fulfillment: *Ten Goals You Must Pursue to Lead a Balanced Life!*	$7.95		
...ailure & Progress: *A Powerful Performance Acceleration Strategy*	$7.95		
The Power of Focus: *Your Future Depends Upon It!*	$7.95		
The Ten Commandments of Goal-Setting: *Violate Them at Your Own Risk!*	$7.95		
Goal Setting 101: *How to Set and Achieve a Goal*	$7.95		
Goal-Setting for Knuckleheads: *Quick and Easy Guidance for the Goal-Impaired*	$7.95		
Rhythm & Flow: *Finding Your Optimal Performance Groove*	$7.95		
Think! *How to Use Your Mind to Achieve Your Goals*	$7.95		
Mind Munchies: *A Delicious Assortment of Brain Snacks*	$7.95		
Mentors & Protegés: *How to Select, Manage, and Lead Dynamic Relationships*	$7.95		
Personal Goal Planner (12 Pack)	$19.95		
Personal Goal Planner (Single Copy)	$2.95		
Reading Journal: *Your Personal Record of Quotations, Reflections, and Impressions*	$8.95		
Goal Setting Forms: *Tools to Help You Get Ready, Get Set, & Go For Your Goals!*	$14.95		
Goals Journal: *A Record of My Life's Accomplishments*	$14.95		
Countdown Clock	$24.95		
Top Ten Goals – Post It Notes (Six Pack)	$9.95		
Top Ten Goals – Post It Notes (Twelve Pack)	$14.95		
Goal Setting Trilogy	$19.95		
Goal Setting Starter Kit	$89.95		
Personal Board of Directors: *Your Team of Trusted Advisors*	$19.95		
Personal Balance Profile: *Charting Your Current Reality*	$19.95		
Personal Mission Statement: *Defining Your Life's Purpose*	$19.95		
Personal Branding: *Creating Brand You!*	$19.95		
Personal Strategic Plan: *Your Blueprint for Success*	$19.95		

Transfer your selections to the Order Form or call us at 1-877-GoalsGuy.
Save money by ordering through our website at www.goalsguy.com

☑ Contact me about: ☐ Speaking Services ☐ Training Programs ☐ Coaching for Results

ORDER FORM

Goal Setting 101

How to Set and Achieve a Goal

PRICING SCHEDULE

1-99 copies	$7.95
100 - 249 copies	$7.50
250 - 999 copies	$6.95
1000 - 4999 copies	$6.50
5000+ copies	$6.25

Name _____

Title _____

Company _____

Address _____

City _____ State _____ Zip _____

Phone _____ Ext. _____

Fax _____ E-mail _____

ORDERING INFORMATION	Quantity	Unit Price	Subtotal
Goal Setting 101			
Self Study Guide for Goal Setting 101		$2.95	

SHIPPING & HANDLING

$4.00 for the first item

.50¢ for each additional item.

Please call for overnight and international shipping rates.

Shipping & Handling *See the chart at left*	
State Sales Tax *FL Residents add 7%*	
Total	

PAYMENT METHOD

❏ VISA ❏ MasterCard ❏ American Express ❏ Check Enclosed ❏ Please Invoice

Card # ⬚⬚⬚⬚⬚⬚⬚⬚⬚⬚⬚⬚⬚⬚⬚⬚⬚⬚⬚ Exp. ⬚⬚ / ⬚⬚

ORDERING METHOD

❏ **Toll-Free:** 1-877-GoalsGuy

❏ **Phone:** 315-422-1777

❏ **Fax:** 315-422-1888

❏ **Internet:** www.goalsguy.com

❏ **E-mail:** order@goalsguy.com

❏ **Mail:** The GoalsGuy
376 Grant Blvd., Suite 205
Syracuse, New York 13206

GARY RYAN BLAIR

Gary Ryan Blair is The GoalsGuy, an internationally recognized authority on goal-setting and personal strategic planning. ,ough his speeches, books, and seminars he teaches individuals and organizations how to set goals and design strategies for meaningful lives and legacies.

Gary is the president of GoalsGuy Learning Systems, a highly-specialized training and consulting firm that teaches people of all ages the art of goal-setting. He has created numerous world class products and services which make up The GoalsGuy Library, resources for children, teenagers, college students, and adults.

His personal philosophy can be summarized into two words: Everything Counts! Gary believes and teaches that your every action and thought either moves you toward or away from your goals. That every moment offers an opportunity for advancement or retreat.

Gary has created and sponsored Kids Goals Education Week, a time for kids and teens to learn about goal-setting and its influence on their future. In addition, New Years Resolution Week, an activity rich opportunity for people to begin each new year - purposely!

At the GoalsGuy, Our Goal Is Simply To Help You Achieve Yours!

For information on The GoalsGuy products, training, speaking, and consulting services contact:

GoalsGuy Learning Systems, Inc.
36181 E. Lake Road, Suite 139
Palm Harbor, Florida 34685

Phone: 877-462-5748
Fax: 800-731-4625
Web site: www.goalsguy.com
Email: gary@goalsguy.com